WORSHIP

HILLSONGS AUSTRALIA
LEADERSHIP SERIES

DARLENE ZSCHECH

Worship - Hillsongs Australia Leadership Series
Copyright © 1996 Darlene Zschech
                       Hillsongs Australia

ISBN 0 646 286161

Publisher	Hillsongs Australia
	PO Box 1195 Castle Hill
	NSW 2154 AUSTRALIA
	Phone 61 2 634 7633
	Fax 61 2 899 4591
Cover design by	CPGD
	4 Marguerite Crescent
	West Pennant Hills
	NSW 2125 AUSTRALIA
Printed by	Pirie Printers Pty Limited
	140 Gladstone Street
	(PO Box 438) Fyshwick
	ACT 2609 AUSTRALIA

ACKNOWLEDGEMENTS

I would like thank my wonderful Lord, who 'breathed life into me, and made me whole'.

My precious family, Mark, Amy and Chloé, who continually inspire me and release me to share my love of God with others.

To Brian and Bobbie Houston, and the team at Hills Christian Life Centre - I am ever thankful that our destinies united.

To the team at Hillsongs Australia, and especially Simone Ridley for so many hours of typing and laughter.

To Graeme Kirkwood and Ruth Grant, thank you so much.

To all the precious singers and muso's at Hills - I thank God for each one of you and your desire to serve Him.

CONTENTS

SHOUT TO THE LORD

My Jesus, my Saviour
Lord there is none like You
All of my days, I want to praise
The wonders of Your mighty love

My comfort, my shelter
Tower of refuge and strength
Let every breath, all that I am
Never cease to worship You

Shout to the Lord
All the earth let us sing
Power and majesty, Praise to the King
Mountains bow down
And the seas will roar
At the sound of Your name

I sing for joy
At the work of Your hand
Forever I'll love You, Forever I'll stand
Nothing compares to the promise
I have in You

INTRODUCTION

John 4:23-24
"The time is coming when the true worshippers will worship the Father in spirit and truth, and that time is here already. You see, the Father too is actively seeking such people to worship Him. God is Spirit and those who worship Him, must worship in spirit and truth."

'Shout To The Lord' which I wrote in 1993, is a song that many people have sung throughout the world and has been recorded many, many times. This by far exceeded my expectations. In fact when I first wrote it, it took me twenty minutes to work up the courage to present it to the team. The words purely reflect the awesomeness of God and my worship to Him. Many people have commented that it has helped them to further their intimacy in worshipping God, but be reminded, it is only a song. Your personal relationship with God is the most important thing.

Worship is not about great songs or great musicianship. It is about you, your heart and your relationship with God. It is an act of pure adoration, where above all else, in all circumstances, even without wonderful voices, instruments, latest technology, with all the highs, the lows, trials, successes - whatever is happening in our lives we will worship God, the King of Kings, my closest friend, the Saviour of our lives.

This book is not designed to tell you the only way to use your gifts in worship. It is intended as a practical help, loaded with different ideas which I have come across so far on this journey.

I am sure that as you read this book and as you 'live life', you can add more chapters and fill in your own gaps, but remember unless you make a start you'll never move forward.

I pray this is a blessing to you.

CHAPTER ONE

CREATED TO
WORSHIP

Never underestimate the power of
worship,
of spending time in the presence of God.

I love to share on the subject of worship, for no other reason than because I LOVE TO WORSHIP GOD!!

You either worship God or you worship creation, there is no middle ground. Every man, woman and child has been created to worship something - you choose. It is not just a movement of the mind, but a rich and complex action, which consumes your very nature. It affects the way you live your life.

There is so much to learn in any area of ministry and just when you think you've got it down, God starts to work on another area!!

I have been singing and performing since I was ten years old, in fact my life has been full of music and expression for as long as I can remember. It is such a part of who I am. Even my parents met while going to a musical rehearsal - it goes very deep!!

I can still remember going to my first music practice at my church. I was a brand new christian, and very excited about meeting christian musicians and playing christian music. I knew it was going to be just like heaven!!

When I arrived I noticed that even though the people were beautiful, when they started to play and sing, everyone became inward and very serious. I tried to fit in with the crowd, to be the same as everyone around me. I tried not to laugh too much and enjoy myself in case they thought I wasn't spiritual. Eventually it happened at 16 years of age - I became a church singer.

It has taken years for God to teach me to be myself. I mustn't be ashamed of the things which make me who I am, but rather be available for God to use me, even if I am very much a 'works in progress'.

The one thing that God keeps saying to me is . . . worship in Spirit and in truth, in other words, be yourself. The wonderful thing about God is that He created each of us as individuals, unique and very special, to accomplish His purpose for our life.

Isaiah 43:7
"Bring to Me all the people who are Mine, whom I made for My glory, whom I formed and made."

As worship leaders, singers and musicians, you should get so excited at the absolute honour of leading people, from all walks of life into His presence. It is such a privilege.

Church is the gathering of the saints together, where as one, we can corporately honour our Lord and Saviour. Always remember that church is not an enemy. It is a vehicle for seeing unsaved people receive Christ as Lord. A body of people who join together, raise their hands and worship God.

Colossians 3:14-15
"Do all these things; but most important, love each other. Love is what holds you all together in perfect unity. Let the peace that Christ gives control your thinking, because you were all called together in one body to have peace."

It makes me laugh that musicians and singers, involved in some churches, are starting to form little unions to protect themselves from becoming overworked and underpaid. They are totally forgetting that God has not called us to be Christian personalities but rather, to be servants of Christ - with no conditions or unnecessary agendas.

Matthew 6:33
"Seek ye first the Kingdom of God, and His righteousness, and all of these things shall be added unto you."

When you worship, the Holy Spirit can speak and be heard. Worship enables your heart to be open to receive.

We exalt the Lord, Who was, and Who is and is to come - we embrace His word and His promises.

1 Chronicles 16:27
"Splendor and majesty are before Him, strength and joy in His dwelling place."

Isaiah 12:2-3
"Surely God is my salvation, I will trust and not be afraid. The Lord, the Lord, is my strength and my song, He has become my salvation. With joy you will draw water from the wells of salvation."

These scriptures are so full of the grace of God. As we worship our Father and spend time in His presence, the promise is that "STRENGTH AND JOY" are found in His dwelling place. If there is anything we need today, it is strength and joy. Not the natural form the world offers, but the deep joy and incredible strength that is only found in God's presence.

When Paul and Silas were in jail, they worshipped God. They knew He would never fail them. Suddenly, while they were worshipping there came an incredible sound, breaking through all natural barriers, and God delivered them from that prison. Again and again, the Bible gives us powerful examples of strength and joy being evident as the children of the living God rise up and worship Him!!!

Worship is a positive act. It's essence is something given, not given up, a free will offering which embodies and reflects the selfless generosity of God. True sacrifice is always an act of generosity - the giving of your self. Without it, worship can easily degenerate into emotional admiration.

Paul and Silas were definitely not just lost in the happiness of the moment, - there was not too much to be happy about at the time, but they had faith in their God! They were really worshipping and praising God.

We were created to worship, spend time in the presence of God. It doesn't just give us a quick fix, and a feel good session. This is not the newest 'self-help manual'!! Literally, the Spirit of God starts to change us from the inside as we learn to open ourselves up to Him and what He is saying to us.

There is a beautiful hymn that was written in 1874 by Horatio G Spafford, a Chicago based lawyer who was renowned for his Godly lifestyle and Christian activities.

This story was recorded by DL Moody and Ira D Sankey, well known evangelists of the day, while they were holding meetings in Edinburgh in 1874.

When telling the story Ira Sankey said We heard of the sad news of the loss of the French steamer Ville de Havre, on her return from America to France. On board was his wife Mrs Spafford, with her four children. In mid ocean a collision took place with a sailing vessel, causing the steamer to sink in only half an hour. Nearly all on board were lost.

Mrs Spafford had hurriedly taken her children from their berths and up on deck. Knowing the steamer was rapidly sinking, she knelt down with her children in prayer. She asked God that they might be saved if possible or made ready to die if it was His will.

In a few minutes the vessel sank and the children were lost. One of the sailors of the vessel, while rowing in a lifeboat over the spot where the steamer had disappeared, discovered Mrs Spafford floating in the water.

He rescued her and ten days later she landed safely at Cardiff from where she cabled her husband the message: 'SAVED ALONE'.

Immediately upon receiving his wife's message, Horatio Spafford started for England to bring her home to Chicago.

DL Moody left his meeting in Edinburgh and went to try to comfort the bereaved parents. It was in commemoration of the death of his children, that Horatio Spafford wrote the hymn which has brought comfort to many a troubled heart. This is how it opens:

> *"When peace, like a river, attendeth my way*
> *When sorrows, like sea-billows, roll;*
> *Whatever my lot, Thou hast taught me know,*
> *It is well, it is well with my soul."*

How is your soul? Is it well? How is your heart? Does it leap to defend the things of God? Or does it leap to defend the things that concern you and your best interests? In Matthew 6:21, Jesus says your heart will be where your treasure is.

Look at David's Prayer . . .

1 Chronicles 29:17-18
"I know, my God, that You test people's hearts. You are happy when people do what is right. I was happy to give all these things, and I gave with an honest heart. Your people gathered here are happy to give to You, and I rejoice to see their giving. Lord, You are the God of our ancestors the God of Abraham, Isaac, and Jacob. Make Your people want to serve You always, and make them want to obey You."

In the Psalms . . .

"Sing all you whose hearts are right"

"And David led them with an innocent heart and guided them with skillful hands"

"Light shines on those who do right, joy belongs to those who are honest"

"God, examine me and know my heart, test me and know my thoughts"

"He heals the brokenhearted and bandages their wounds"

Worship is about your heart. Keep it healthy, for out of it do indeed come the true issues of life. If your heart is healthy, your soul will thrive!!

'My strength and my song'.

Recently I was in a meeting at a great church in Texas leading praise and worship. My attention was drawn to a particular young couple who, throughout worship, were visibly glowing and basking in the glory of God.

Their faces were radiant. They seemed to be worshipping God with everything they had. I wanted to meet them. When we did meet, I asked them about their love for God and to share something of their testimony with me. They held hands and related how just six weeks earlier they had lost their five week old baby to cot death. That was not what I was expecting to hear!!!

They were living, breathing testimonies of *Exodus 15:2: 'the Lord is my strength and my song'*. Their faith and worship were a declaration of God's power and Lordship over their lives. Through their attitude of praise God was able to minister to them and hold their lives together.

I will never forget this family. Their testimony and uncompromising faith in God has stirred and challenged the lives of many Christians. We are created to worship. It is an incredible step of faith when your world is falling apart.

This couple's testimony has also helped inspire me to keep writing songs to uplift and encourage the family of God. If you are obedient to God and the gift on your life, you never know how God may use you.

When we start to sing and praise God, we are choosing to lay all things aside, to lift up our hands, to open our hearts and confess the life we have found in Christ.

Psalm 138:2
"I will worship toward Your holy temple and praise Your name for Your loving kindness and Your truth. For You have magnified Your word above all Your name."

All the troubles that can be thrown on you in life pale into insignificance when compared to the promises of God. It is powerful to actually vocalize these promises and let your spirit and soul rise above to the level where the heart of God says - it's OK - trust Me - have faith in Me and My ability, not yourself or your ability.

Many of you would be able to pin point times in your life when you have made a decision to, 'Praise the Lord' and 'Worship Him' - despite your circumstance. There is such strength in this!! This is where faith comes into its own in your life. And when you are full of faith - your life will overflow with miraculous testimonies of the greatness of God.

There have been many times in my life when, as I started singing and praising God in the midst of a hard time, the Holy spirit has literally come and 'lifted me up' above my circumstance. To rise up and worship the living God, this is what we were created to do.

I have seen God use my faith, meet me halfway and turn a trial into an opportunity to testify of His faithfulness.

I clearly remember one morning, just after my father passed away, I was hanging out the washing (some things in life just never change!!) and my heart was breaking.

My father was a wonderful man and even though I knew he was now 'dancing with the angels' - I missed him so much I found it hard to breathe.

So I started to sing, just quietly to myself, "To God be the Glory", (one of my fathers favourite songs) - God's presence filled my life, just standing outside my little home, with my two year old running around by my feet.

There was such a healing in my heart that day.

Created to Worship Jesus - what a gift!

The worship songs and hymns we sing are not christian jingles or 'ditties'. They are words of life, full of faith and hope. They reflect the heart of God for His children. They inspire us with statements like:

> *'When mountains fall, I'll stand, by the power of your hand, and in your heart of hearts I'll dwell, and that my soul knows very well'.*

I have received many letters from people who have been placed in tragic situations, and through a worship song, have been powerfully ministered to.

Melodies and music have a dynamic ability to involve your soul - to connect with your heart, emotions and mind. When they are saturated with the anointing of God, they become a powerful tool which, when used effectively and not manipulatively, become an incredible blessing.

You can never underestimate God's holiness, power and divinity in your life or on the ministry of worship.

The more time we spend in God's presence worshipping Him, the more we begin to hear and know His voice. His power becomes real and evident in our lives and we become more like Jesus.

CHAPTER TWO

POWER OF PRAISE AND WORSHIP

When people see the presence of God in your life, they will run towards salvation.

Worship is not based on a formula or set of rules. We are individuals, created so uniquely that to put God into 'Our worship experience box' is missing it. Churches and individuals around the world worship in so many different ways, and yet most of the time, the result is still the same. If our hearts and motives are pure, we exalt God and not ourselves.

The word worship actually means, *to bow down, to reverence, to fall flat . . .*

Revelation 1:17, "and when I saw Him I fell at His feet as dead." When we praise God, we thank Him for what He has done, what He is going to do, for what He has done in our lives, but when we worship God, we worship who He is, King of Kings, not just for what He can do for us. *2 Corinthians 3:18 . . . "We are changed into the same image from glory to glory. . ."*

Worship encompasses our spiritual lives, our physical lives, our social lives and the giving of our tithes and offerings. God needs all of us not just 50%!! Worship is our life.

When we praise God, we celebrate what He has done for us and what He continues to do. Then we often enter a time of intimate worship adoring God for Who He is, His holiness, His splendour, acknowledging that He is the Great I Am.

Praise and worship takes on many different characteristics. The following is a list of some of these:

1. To Celebrate and Exalt.
2. To Evangelise and Share the Gospel.
3. Warfare.
4. Healing.
5. Seeking God.

1. To Celebrate and Exalt.

Don't confine fast songs to praise and slow songs to worship. The word speaks of "joy unspeakable and full of glory", celebrating our God. Sometimes when you are lost in worship you just want to raise your voice, lift your hands, throw your head back, dance and rejoice, purely because you are in God's presence.

I'm not talking happy, clapping Pentecostal (don't be offended, that's me!). I'm talking about spending time with your Maker. You will never be the same again.

The Message Bible says this:

"I'm happy from the inside out, and from the outside in, I'm firmly formed. You cancelled my tickets to hell - that's not my destination! Now you've got my feet on the life path, all radiant from the shining of Your face. Ever since You took my hand, I'm on the right way."

We have so much to celebrate!

The word exaltation, speaks of a raising of the heart, the voice, the hands. It means *to increase, to exalt above, to lift up high, to rejoice . . .* This basically says it all.

Psalm 99:9
"Exalt the Lord our God and worship at His Holy mountain."

To Adore our God.

I love reading in Revelation 5:13 when John writes: *"then I heard every creature in heaven and earth, in under world and sea join in, all voices, in all places, singing. To the One on the throne, to the Lamb, the blessing, the honour, the glory, the strength, for age after age after age."*

The magnificence of this moment would have been so difficult to translate into words - What a sound! All voices, in all places. Total adoration!

To adore someone is an unusual expression. It is a word that I find myself using more and more to express my love for God. Sometimes 'love' just does not say all I want to say.

2. To Evangelise and Share the Gospel.

Did I mention back on page 7 that when Paul and Silas worshipped in jail, the jailer ended up giving his life to Christ?!

When people see the presence of God in your life, they will run towards salvation. When people see singing and making noise for noise sake, people will be put off. *1 Corinthians 13* speaks of having many gifts, but if we do not have love, these gifts don't amount to much at all. *"If I do not have love, I am only a noisy bell or a clashing cymbal."*
1 Corinthians 13:1

The world is full of counterfeits and even though we live in this world we have taken on a different spirit to this world. Remember who you represent. When you worship in truth, people are drawn towards Christ.

To dance, sing or play with perfection is no good if you can't reflect the love of Christ through who you are!

When you open your life up to the power of God and sing His praise, proclaiming His might, you are setting yourself up for a mighty move of the Holy Ghost.

3. Warfare.

The enemy has no chance in the middle of people who are consumed by the presence of God. Can you believe that in 2 Chronicles 20:20 the Word says *"Jehoshaphat stood and said, 'Listen to me Judah and people of Jerusalem! Have faith in the Lord your God and you will be upheld.'"*

Then he appointed men to praise Him for the splendor of His holiness as they went out ahead of the army saying *"give thanks to the Lord for His love endures forever." 2 Chronicles 20:21*

As they began to sing and praise, the Lord God delivered them as He promised and they defeated the enemy. Be encouraged, the battle is not yours - it is the Lords.

This all applies to you and me. Don't be naive, if you are impacting lives for Christ, you are a target for the enemy. The good news is that God holds the keys of hell and death, the devil is defeated. There is power in the name of Jesus, there is power in praise and worship!

4. Healing.

Do you know that one of the Greek words for worship is "<u>therapeuo</u>" which means *to cure and to heal.* There have been many times over the last few years, during worship, someone has brought a prophetic song, bringing words of life, comfort, and healing.

1Samuel 16:23
"Whenever the spirit from God came upon Saul, David would take his harp and play. Then relief would come to Saul: He would feel better, and the evil spirit would leave him."

When Saul was very ill David would take his harp and play. The scripture actually says that Saul would feel better and the evil spirit would leave him as David played and ministered healing to him.

Words of life that are played and sung have ministered healing to my soul many times - it is not the song that ministers, it is the anointing on that song that breathes life where maybe there was none.

5. Seeking God.

The more we seek Him, the more we spend time with Him, the more we want to know Him.

As worshippers you will:
- Minister to God in His presence.
- See God move mightily in His church.
- Watch God change you from the inside out!

Here is one of my favourite scriptures on seeking the Lord. Let these truths invade your life.

Psalm 27:4-6
"One thing I ask of the Lord, this is what I seek: that I may dwell in the house of the Lord, all the days of my life, to gaze upon the beauty of the Lord and to seek Him in His temple. For in the day of trouble he will keep me safe in His dwelling, He will hide me in the shelter of His tabernacle and set me high upon a rock. Then my head will be exalted above the enemies who surround me; at His tabernacle will I sacrifice with shouts of joy; I will sing and make music to the Lord."

28

Worship is a verb, not a noun.
It's not only what you say, it is what you do.

Worship is a lifestyle, not just a Sunday thing. Your thoughts, your actions and reactions are often a clear indication of a life of worship. It is a selfless lifestyle which, focuses on the ways of God, not on what 'I' think. A life of service, a life of giving. Jesus' whole life was a single act of worship. **And God so graciously makes this life readily accessible to us.**

We are just scratching the surface when talking about worship and its effects on your life, but you can not deny its power and purpose in your life.

CHAPTER THREE

THE WORSHIP TEAM

Being a valued member of your team
should not be a requirement -
make it the love of your life!!

At the moment, Praise and Worship is very popular, and successful formulas are becoming the rage. It almost seems as though if you don't have the huge choir and the latest look that maybe your church is doing something wrong. God doesn't need props. There is really only one thing you need to qualify for being on any part of God's team, and that is to BE AVAILABLE.

If you believe the Bible, then you believe in the team! Jesus Himself had a team which turned the world upside down.

The Collins Dictionary says:
Team: *a group of people willingly committed to a common goal.*

Team is an attitude, not something that you do. Team is more than a group of people working together. It is people sold out to a defined purpose committed to its fulfillment throughout it's conception, pregnancy, birth, life and death.

On your own, you can only do so much! It is wonderful watching how God puts people together uniting their gifts and multiplying their effectiveness.

You can have a team that looks great with all the right people in place, but again, without a vision and common goal, strong leadership, great teaching, they will eventually fall over, and certainly never become an effective organism!

Can you stop for a moment and think about how many times you've strived and tried to do things, fulfill dreams, on your own, and were left feeling frustrated? Or been part of a so-called team, whose interests were really not in the corporate effectiveness but in their own gain?

Psalm 133:3 says that when we are united, God commands a blessing! There is power in team.

In your worship team, be there for the right reasons.

Church is not a vehicle for you to present your talents and catapult you into Christian stardom.

Be the best team player ever.

- Be COMMITTED to the success of your fellow team players.
- As a team player, you should know where the team is going. Know your church's VISION, learn the songs. Be a valued player.
- Team members SHARPEN each other, like iron sharpens iron. Sometimes sparks fly!! But I am reminded that:
    1. We're not called to serve man, we're called to serve God.
    2. I believe God places us with certain people to stretch us, mould us, to build each other into the people we're meant to be!

GREAT TEAM MEMBERS ARE LOYAL - TO THE TEAM AND EACH OTHER!!!!

Australian Concise Oxford Dictionary
Loyal: *true, faithful, to duty, love or obligation. Faithful in allegiance.*

Love Christ, have God first in your life. Be on God's team because you love Jesus and are loyal to Him.

I am kidding myself if I think that what God is doing in my life, is because of me. All I am, is available and committed to seeing peoples' lives changed through Jesus Christ!!

Commitment does take hard work, but this is not a 'labour of love', this is what we are created to do. Commitment is team and team means commitment.

Perhaps you don't feel adequate to be part of your church music team. Perhaps you have been to many church meetings and left determined to change and improve your life. Yet so quickly, you find your determination waning away at just the time you need to or should be putting into practice the very words you heard.

It is at this point you put yourself on an emotional roller coaster. "I'm not good enough" - "I'll never get better" - "How can I be like him/her" - "I can't even think about the mountains further down the road 'cause I keep getting stuck on the same old speed hump."

How do you get off this up and down, up and down roller coaster? As singers and muso's, sometimes our nature or personality tends to have major swings.
Are you happy with this?
Do you want to change?
Can God use you to your best if some days you are hot and others you are not?

I think this will help you . . .

Any decision or resolution is simply a promise to yourself which is worth nothing unless you have your sights genuinely set on God's best. You need to turn this decision into a habit. You cannot make this decision into a habit unless it is linked to a life purpose.

What is your life purpose?

To achieve greatness for God? Make a difference in
this world? Raise a strong Christian family?
Releasing some of your team into their potential in
God? - or whatever else you want to fill in . . . Make
these kind of decisions your habit every day. Look
at your life purpose. You will be well on the high
road that God has intended for you, the leader in
your own life, in control of your strengths and
weaknesses. This is why having a life purpose is so
important for your future and that of your team.

This is a true story of a young man named William
H. Murray who, through commitment and the
revelation of what God could do, changed the lives
of many people.

In 1852 when William was only nine years old, he
caught his arm in a large wheel playing at his fathers
sawmill. Unfortunately it had to be amputated. His
father's dream of taking over his business was
shattered and his neighbours commented **"all his
chances in life are gone, for what can a cripple
boy do?"**

William continued going to school and when he had finished he became a postman. William had ten sisters and had to earn his own income somehow. Even with his crippled arm he had a great love for people and his great dream was to become a missionary. Over and over he applied to the Bible Society, but they preferred strong able bodied men for the physical job of carrying Bibles into overseas countries.

William trusted God, his passion was not limited to his physical body and his sense of Destiny and Mission for God's sake was beyond measure. As he delivered the mail he constantly prepared himself with the belief that one day God would make a way. Meanwhile he studied the Bible, Hebrew, Greek and hungered after God.

At last a door had opened and at the age of twenty he was sent by the Bible Society to sell Bibles at the Glasgow Docks. At these docks the sailors attached themselves to this one armed Bible seller and the Bible Society found him to be the best salesman they had ever had. Eventually several of these sailors offered to pay for William's Bible College fees.

William's daily lifestyle while at Bible College went something like this:

3.00am - 8.00am	Study for College
8.00am - 10.00am	College Lectures
10.00am - 6.00pm	Sell Bibles
6.00pm	Went Home

I am sure that there were days when he had to draw on that inner strength of Destiny and continually control his attitude to sustain and encourage him during this part of his life. His life purpose was still before him. For seven years he followed the above schedule with an excellence and a passion to do his best. His predominant thought was "whatever it takes".

He was finally sent as a missionary to China and began to learn the 4,000 strange and difficult characters in which the Bible was printed for the Chinese people.

Some people would say that William's life was more that most could handle, but William was only just starting.

Not by chance or fate, but destiny, William met many blind men on his travels and his desire to teach them the Bible became his life passion.

Many days and nights he spent thinking and praying about how he could teach these blind men to read the Bible. With 4,000 characters and the 480 sounds of the Chinese language it was not going to be easy. He invented a system that could teach this language to these blind people in less than three months (it takes several years to learn Chinese for sighted people).

William was on a mission from God. As his next step, he generously donated all his personal savings to house, feed, clothe and teach one old man and two orphan boys (these were William's first students). After they learned to read using his new system, the school expanded to nine students - it became literally the blind teaching the blind.

Since those early days of renting an extra room for his first students he bought several buildings and started many schools, sending blind Chinese missionaries across China in the middle of the Boxer Rebellion, having a major impact for the Kingdom of God.

For many years, William H. Murray could be seen on the streets of Peking, selling Bibles and preaching Christ to the people in the streets. His passion was neither exhausted or curtailed but with that sense of destiny he continues to live every day.

Imagine how the effectiveness of your music team would improve if every single one of them had a revelation of their life purpose. A sense of destiny and purpose like that of William H. Murray.

Being a valued member of your team should not be a requirement, but a privilege. Make it the love of your life!!

The question we have to ask ourselves is . . . What cost are we willing to pay?

Our answer must be very clear because when the times of pressure and challenge are on us, we need inner strength to carry us through, because our pastor's passion or our leader's vision will not do it. Remember William's motto . . . "whatever it takes". That's what it costs to fulfil our life's purpose. Whatever it takes.

Your motto should read . . .
"Whatever the cost - pressing forward - 'till it's finished"

Raising Up Leaders.

Matthew 9:37-38
"Jesus said to his Followers, 'There are many people to harvest but only a few workers to help harvest them. Pray to the Lord, who owns the harvest, that He will send more workers to gather the harvest.'"

If you are a Team Leader, it is your responsibility to do yourself out of a job!! To equip people to follow you. It sounds crazy!! But I am only doing my job if I succeed in raising up and training the next level of leaders. In fact I should train them to do the job as well, if not better than I. This is easier said than done especially since most of us link our self worth and identity to what we do.

I personally have felt this in recent times. As God is taking me and leading me on I must continue to literally let go of some of the things that I love to do and naturally do well. The hardest thing is letting go when you don't know for sure exactly where the next step will take you. This means I have to activate my faith and trust God.

44

It's like the trapeze artist. There is a moment in time when, as they let go of the bar, they are suspended in mid-air with only the hope, faith and trust that their partner will be there to grab them before they fall.

I know what this feels like.

Being a leader takes strength, commitment, faith and hard work. There is a cost, there is a risk. But when you see people following you, their lives enriched and blessed, it is more than worth it.

When God is calling, you follow.

THE TEAM PLAYERS

The Music Director (MD).

The music pastor and 'legend song writer' at our church, Russell Fragar, says this ......

The Music Director's role is to translate the wishes of the worship leader into direction for the musicians. Obviously he or she needs to be able to both lead the band, and be able to see, hear and inwardly feel what the worship Leader needs, and then bring them together.

This happens best when there are great personal relationships and one united purpose - to worship God together, free of personal agendas. We always try to prefer one another in love, and God seems to bless that.

The key words that describe our relationships are love, respect, giving and commitment.

If you read through 1 and 2 Chronicles you'll see that all the chief musicians in the Old Testament were appointed and given awesome Godly authority and responsibility. Their roles, as they are today, were not to play the coolest instrument, cross their fingers and then hope that people would follow. It was and is a ministry that requires you to gather different players with different talents and temperaments and bring a unity and common goal to be in worship and to see God.

Music is a great vehicle to give voice to our emotions. As the Director of music you have the unique opportunity to skillfully create an atmosphere through music which leads people into God's presence with ease and confidence.

As a worship leader it is wonderful to work with MD's who:

- Are there to achieve the same result you are.
- Follow your lead and cover for you if you make a mistake.
- Are committed to each of the band members and interested in seeing them excel without being threatened.
- Are worshippers who know how to lead worship from their instrument.
- Are people in tune with the Holy Spirit and desperate to see the presence of God fall.

We need strong leaders, who lead with a commitment to seeing the music team fulfill the vision of the church. Not the other way around. Yes, your pastor can encourage you, support you, help build you into the person you're meant to be, release you etc etc, but remember you are there first to be a blessing, then the blessing will come to you.

I am fortunate to work with wonderful musicians and Music Directors, who are not only talented, but committed to everyone around them. I have watched and continue to watch in amazement, as God honours them in so many ways!

If you think you can't possibly fulfill this role, and maybe at your church it is really needed, then great! God specializes in people who 'can't do it! Look at this . . .

2 Corinthians 12:9-10
"'My grace is enough for you. When you are weak, My power is made perfect in you.' So I am very happy to brag about my weaknesses. Then Christ's power can live in me. For this reason I am happy when I have weaknesses, insults, hard times, sufferings, and all kinds of troubles for Christ. Because when I am weak, then I am truly strong."

My great friend David Holmes who is the Music Director of Christian City Church, Oxford Falls, wrote the following paragraph on worship. His words are very sincere and anyone who knows Dave and his wife Margie, will know that this is not just a lovely quote. This is literally their testimony and life:

Worship is a lifestyle. It's what we do everyday of our lives as we walk in relationship and friendship with Jesus.

When we are in His presence our hearts and thoughts are transformed and renewed by the Holy Spirit enabling us to understand and relate to our God in a greater way. Whether we sing or play an instrument, what we do is affected by the state of our hearts. Our gifts will be empowered and enriched as we allow the Holy Spirit to work with us in our chosen fields of service. Our desire should be to offer God our best efforts and skills and to honour Him with excellence. When we play with both skill and integrity He will use what we do to change and touch the lives of people.

God bless

David Holmes

The Singers (Backing Vocals).

Vocals are my passion. The singers I'm talking about here are the more confident, up front singers who really undergird and assist whoever is leading worship.

These people need to be fairly strong singers, able to sing solo with purpose, to harmonise. They need to provide a security blanket for the worship leader and to be their voice if they are not a strong singer and especially if they are not a singer at all. These guys need to be on the alert, always watching the worship leader and anticipating their every move. This can be difficult for singers when the worship leader fails to communicate. We'll talk more about that later ...

I've always seen the role of backing vocalist in any situation to be someone who makes the front person look and sound better. They need to be sensitive to the Holy Spirit and to what God is doing in the environment or service they are singing in.

Psalm 33:3
"Sing to the Lord a new song PLAY WELL and joyfully".

It really helps to be skilled. You don't need to be Luther Vandross or Natalie Cole, just continually yearning for knowledge and perfecting your gift. I'm constantly reading about people who are being greatly used by God and being effective in the kingdom. One thing in particular comes through loud and clear: they are all teachable and hungry for wisdom.

In order to continually work on our craft, we do need to learn to let 'the gift' go a little. Don't hold onto it too tight!!

What does that mean? It means learning to listen to criticism, and take what you can from it. That does not mean, let people dump on you, it just means, don't be over sensitive!! Relax!! We all need to continually be growing, both physically, mentally and spiritually. You will never do it if you are offended too easily!!

I was severely pulled into line a few years ago by a wonderful singing teacher whom I admired and was a little scared of (she was tough!!).

After a few weeks of lessons, she asked me to sing an old Beatles' tune and at the end I felt I had done alright. She walked over to the piano and slammed the lid shut!! (This was not quite the reaction I expected).

"I can tell you are a church singer!" she roared (Whoah, this was not meant as a compliment!).

"You've been told too many times that you're good and you have stopped working. You have a lot of work to do young lady . . . !!!"

I wasn't sure what to do, (crying did not seem the appropriate thing to do at the time although that's what I felt like doing) and hearing the truth was a really hard option. I decided to learn from it, put my head down and work hard.

I have thought a lot about that comment many times over the last couple of years and it has proven to be very true.

In church, we are surrounded by a huge embracing family who, after you've sung great or not so great, will say, "Oh darling, that was beautiful, God really blessed me during your singing" or whatever. Now, don't misunderstand me, God uses a willing heart, but never take this blessing and anointing on your gift for granted.

Work on your gifts, go for your best, not anyone else's best, but your best, today.

It is amazing how quickly you can improve your voice, musicianship, playing etc by being diligent in rehearsing.

Philippians 1:10
"That you may approve the things that are excellent, that you may be sincere and without offense till the day of Christ."

Don't be afraid of excellence.

This word usually brings to mind performance and striving. But the most beautiful thing about this scripture is that it says be EXCELLENT but then also says be SINCERE. You can't separate the two. One without the other usually causes frustration.
Ron Kenoly's video "Sing Out with One Voice" is a wonderful example of excellence combined with sincerity. The music is well rehearsed, well choreographed, beautifully presented, well produced and the heart of God is all over it.

Vocal Care.

Your voice is an instrument which requires daily maintenance if you want to use it at full capacity for the long haul. The ideal is to find a great teacher, be disciplined enough to go every week and to practice daily. You've got to remember that you are not a machine. Like it or not, your voice, like any other muscles in the body need exercise and rest. (Tahiti sounds nice!!)

You need to drink a lot of water - one to two litres a day. Sleep is very important. Lack of it not only puts stress on your voice production but also affects your pitch and accuracy.

Avoid straining and shouting (parents take note). Treat your voice with care. If you find you have frequent recurrent voice problems, talk to your voice teacher or speech pathologist who can correct your harmful habits.

On a technical level, most singers when working quite hard on their voices can achieve 80% of their own personal capacity and fail to push through to achieve that last 20%. It's the 20% and not the 80% which will make your voice outstanding rather than great.

To achieve greatness as a musician or a singer, it doesn't just take time, it takes care.

If you've ever heard me speak on vocals you would have heard me speak of 'the mysteries'. Sunday morning at 10.00 am is not the place to find out your early morning vocal capacity. If I'm going to work out what my voice can and can't do, I want it to be in the privacy of my own home. When you get up in church and sing a song and you know that there is one long, big, high, huge note coming up and you are unprepared and unrehearsed for it, you actually short change the rest of the song. You are so worried about that one dreaded bit, that it occupies your thoughts, and the only thing you leave people with is "Boy I felt sorry for that young girl, when she didn't hit that note, she looked really nervous".

Eliminate the mysteries, it will free you up to think about what you are singing about and express it wholeheartedly.

The world says the more work you put in the more you get back, which is quite true, but I like to say the more work you put in, the more you have to give, the more you have to deposit.

If I had the choice between listening over a period of time to a technically perfect singer with no passion or a singer who had a few flaws but was full of heart, I would go for the second singer every time.

Your talent and gift will open doors and get you places, but a heart and passion for what you do will sustain you. You can only operate out of the gift that is on you for a limited amount of time. Go for the gift that is within you.

Proverbs 22:29
"Do you see people skilled in their work? They will work for Kings not ordinary people."

Recently I was singing at a session surrounded by outstanding singers who were excellent at their craft!! (They are all great people, they just don't know God yet.) Afterwards, I went and sat in my car and cried out to God, "Why on earth am I doing this? Why am I here?" Sometimes at work you don't get a chance to share much, but you do get the chance to live out your faith - I knew there had to be more to me being there than just singing!!!

God answered very gently. "You are not among these people for what you can do... You are here for who you are!!"

Let 'who you are' come through whenever you are singing, let the love of Christ shine through you.

I remember one day, Pastor Michael Murphy was talking about how as a Christian, you should make every opportunity in life, work, home, church etc. 'a golden moment' and not to let any opportunity pass you by. That doesn't mean bashing people with your Bible and its principles!! It means, living it!

Wherever you are, live through Jesus - His ways are much higher, and much more satisfying than anything you try and do yourself!

Presentation.

When it comes to visuals, and how you present yourself, here are a few guidelines:

- Be guided by the standards your leader has set.
- Be neat and tidy.
- In worship, make sure your attire is not a distraction.
- Try not to see how close to the edge you can go eg modesty, fashion. Be wise.

I'm always joking with our guys about presentation, the latest saying is . . . If it still moves, gaff it down!!

Colossians 3:16
"Let the teaching of Christ live in you richly. Use all wisdom to teach, instruct each other by singing psalms, hymns and spiritual songs with thankfulness in your hearts to God."

The PA.

Be wise when it comes to working with microphones, PA's and your sound team.

There is nothing worse than seeing singers walk in late, pick up their microphone and then complain that they can't hear themselves.

Do you realise that your sound man or team have been there for a long time before you arrived and are always the last to leave, AND receive the smallest amount of attention?

Learn that these people are as much a part of this team as you are, without them, it makes singing REAL HARD.

Last year, at Hillsong Conference, we did a great skit about 'the music rehearsal'!!

There were a small group of players and singers, all looking great, but very unorganised, they had us laughing as we watched them 'cramming' for the service.

Just before the service starts, we had 'the star singer' arriving late, dressed in sequins (remember, we were trying to prove a point!), waltzing in and then doing her thing, regardless of what had previously been 'almost' rehearsed! We had sound men running around, stage guys moving the plants while we were worshipping, the whole crowd were in fits of laughter!

The tragic thing was, when we finally regained our composure, I asked how many people have been in this situation . . . most of them raised their hands. The comments were - "that was too close to the real thing!"

You can either make this very complicated or very simple. Give everything of your talent and **your heart** and God will use you. The scripture that I personally go back to is:

Ephesians 2:10
"God has made us what we are. In Christ Jesus, God made us to do good works, which God planned in advance for us to live our lives doing."

It is no accident that we are part of this ministry, this is our destiny!!

The Muso's.

You guys and gals are not just the backup band. You cannot hide behind the singers or MD. You are worshippers, giving the best of your playing, on your particular instrument.

You:
- Are a valued team player.
- Are punctual to rehearsals (ouch!).
- Learn all the new songs and have folders full of material (well prepared!).
- Accompany the singers in Praise and Worship.
- Musically interpret songs that are sung!
- Participate in the service and don't hide behind your instrument.
- Are confident to worship God on your instrument, even leading the band or soloing if needed.

Plus stacks more!!!

Psalm 150

"Praise the Lord! Praise God in His Temple; praise Him in His mighty heaven. Praise Him for His strength; praise Him for His greatness. Praise Him with trumpet blast; praise Him with harps and lyres. Praise Him with tambourines and dancing; praise Him with stringed instruments and flutes. Praise Him with loud cymbals; Praise Him with crashing cymbals. Let everything that breathes praise the Lord.
Praise the Lord."

In our church, we audition all of the players to see where they are up to and talk to them about their dreams and desires.

We do not use everyone who comes through, although, we do try and encourage them to get lessons, be involved in other areas of Creative Ministries and try again!

There are many areas for your musicians or yourself, to get involved, even if it doesn't mean Sundays. There are mid week services, new christians, youth, women's groups, etc, all of which use up and coming players and singers, to give them training and development first hand.

I have sung with many different musicians and discovered that like the voice, you can only go so far using technique and method. There are times in our worship when I feel that it could just 'take-off' musically. This means lots of passion and soul, but even more it means having discernment, and sensitivity to the dynamics of the meeting.

Our trumpet player, Mark Gregory, would have to be one of the finest communicators on his instrument that I've ever heard. He doesn't miss a beat. Every time I have thought, "I wish the trumpet would lead out now", there it is!!! This is not a skill picked up at the conservatorium . . . this is Holy Spirit stuff.

Watch your MD or those around you, listen to the rest of the band and play as a unit, be spiritually aware as to what God is doing.

Those of you in smaller environments, don't be discouraged. Maybe <u>you are</u> the MD, Worship Leader, in charge of the singers, songwriter and sound man!! A one-man band!! Most of us have been in this situation - remember - every large church began as a small church.

Be faithful in whatever God has given you to do, today! Then He will entrust you with much!

I was speaking at a seminar one day when a young lady asked the question -
"I am the only muso in our church, how do I build a team with only one?"

At first, I wasn't sure what to say as I could sense the frustration in her. I prayed, "God, give me an answer here", and He came up with something I really didn't expect. He said "Tell her to start having rehearsals!"

I thought, No Way - Why would you hold a band practice by yourself? Pretty outside idea, but Hey - God is the best at not doing things the way we think they should be done!

So, I started conveying this to her and it started to make sense. If you need more musicians and you want to lift the standard of your music, you need to have something worthwhile for them to come to.

She started holding rehearsal nights once a week, advertised in the weekly church newsletter and prayed!!

The first three weeks, there she was, by herself, trying to stay excited about what God was doing! (this is called FAITH!)

On the fourth week, you guessed it, a singer and a guitarist turned up and then month by month, God blessed them with a beautiful bunch of people, who had hearts to minister through worship. God is so faithful, His word is true, He always seems to meet us halfway. Step out in faith, and God will honour your commitment and bless it.

Ephesians 4:16 says *'every joint'* supplies the body. When only half the body is operating how it should, unnatural strain is placed on those joints.

But when the whole body is carrying and distributing the weight together, the body flows smoothly, burden is lighter AND more efficient.

As a musician, do you supply or do you just carry your weight?

Don't just do the minimum requirement - be involved because it is your life, because you love God and love to offer Him your worship. Be there wholeheartedly because you want to be part of the sovereign move of God. These are awesome days we live in!

69

Choir.

When we first started the choir it was with much excitement. So we announced to the church that we were starting this wonderful ministry which they could be involved with. That was about five or six years ago. For the first three years the choir averaged between six and (on a huge day) about fifteen people. This was a little disheartening!!

It is very true that *without a vision, the people perish (Proverbs 29:18)* and believe me . . . we were perishing at a fairly great rate!!

Before the choir could move forward and begin entering into their destiny, I had to establish a path for them to follow. As far as personal resource goes, all I had to lead them with was a dream. I felt far too young and inexperienced to lead them, especially as a lot of them were older than me, and had been involved in this area for years.

It's at times like these, when you are feeling unconfident that you need to go back and remember when God clearly called you to fulfill this role. Believe me I've hung onto that moment many times.

I desperately needed to become informed - you can only go so far when you are continually bluffing your way through. I filled my head with CD's of inspirational choirs, watched as many videos I could get my hands on, listened to parts, vocal arrangements and slowly but surely carved a way for them to confidently walk through.

The wonderful thing about a choir is, not just the real 'wall of sound' it creates with flowing harmonies and large degrees of movement in the music. A choir is also an incredible training ground for both talent and character!!

Auditioning.

On a practical level, we audition every singer that comes into our department. We do this for a number of reasons. We don't expect them to be absolutely knockout vocalists, but it does give us a chance to:

- Find out a little bit about the person and where they are at.
- Assess their vocal ability.
- Explain face to face what commitment is expected from them.

Basic requirements for people to pass the audition are:

- Willingness to fulfill the required commitment.
- The ability sing tunefully.
- The ability to show the love of God on their face.

I believe that you can teach most people to sing but the key is teaching them to become great listeners.

One thing that has helped discourage the 'star mentality' for us, has been asking all of our singers, from the most naturally gifted to the ones who have to work harder, to be involved in the choir. Singing as a ministry is vastly different to singing as a career. In church your gift should draw attention to God and His ability, while in the world your gift draws attention to you and your ability.

With CHOIR as the banner of our vocals department any inference that it was secondary to the main vocals has been broken down. Our roles are all different, but our call to serve God is the same!

Having your talent recognised is not wrong. What is wrong is when you join the team purely so your gift will be recognised.

Proverbs 18:16
"A man's gift makes room for him, and brings him before great men." (NASB)

Being part of your ministry team does not mean just showing up and eventually if you work hard, or 'work the system', you'll realise your dreams!! NO WAY!!

Training Ground.

The choir is a wonderful vocal training ground for all levels. It teaches people how to blend well with other singers and how to sing harmonies (most people do not find singing in harmony an easy thing to do).

73

A choir member must learn to work in a close environment with different personalities. They have to learn new songs every week. This always stretches and develops peoples' musicianship to greater levels.

For those who have only ever sung solo, choir is a big change in mindset. However becoming part of a body working together, has advantages (if you are a singer reading this) which far outweigh the discomforts.

A couple of girls came along to Creative Ministries one night whom I knew to be great singers. They had been in 'showbusiness' all their lives. They had sung at the Myer Music Bowl Christmas Spectacular in front of thousands and thousands of people just two months prior. I thought, "What do I do here?" Do I just say "don't worry about choir, I know you're busy" etc, etc? No. Instead, like everybody else, I welcomed them into the worship team through the door of the choir. I have since watched these girls faithfully sow their lives into a greater vision than their own and am excited to see God honour their attitudes day after day.

Section Leaders.

We now have Section Leaders for the Sopranos, Altos and Tenors. These people must know their parts, and help the others learn them.

The responsibility still rests with me though to make sure I know the arrangements and have charts ready for them. If you expect them to come on time and give their all, you must respect them by being prepared.

Roles and Functions.

So why do we use both choir and singers in worship?

CHOIR
To add depth, definition, presence and life to the music. To almost be an anchor for the vocal sound you are trying to produce. To be a training ground for ministries in progress and a constant source of encouragement and support.

We have received many letters from people who have been truly blessed and ministered to by the love of God they have seen represented through the choir. I personally have received many beautiful notes from within the choir sharing how God has taught them so much by learning to be part of a corporate vision.

BACKING SINGERS

I usually place three or four strong vocalists to add clarity to the melody and help the congregation feel confident with the songs. From a visual perspective, they rejoice, lift their hands. Together this encourages the congregation and supports the worship leader.

When you are ministering with people closely, there <u>WILL</u> be personality clashes.

Matthew 5:23-24
"So when you offer your gift to God at the altar, and you remember that your brother or sister has something against you, leave your gift there at the altar. Go and make peace with that person, and then come and offer your gift."

Never let 'niggly' things cloud the state of your heart.

One of the enemy's greatest tactics is to get you side-tracked with subtleties, filling your mind with petty problems, trying to keep your eyes off Jesus.

Don't give in to it.

If there are problems, deal with them and GET UP! Get on with it.

CHAPTER FOUR

WORSHIP LEADERS LOCKS & KEYS

Worship is about man touching God and
God touching man.
David was a man after God's own heart.
He knew how to touch God's heart. He
could make God smile. We must be like
David and actively worship, celebrate, and
receive from God.

Frank Montgomery
Christian Faith Centre - Seattle, USA.

I love leading people into God's presence. I am convinced that it is what I have been created to do.

Worship leading is not something I take lightly. It wasn't something that I just said 'Of course, I can do this!' In fact I didn't think I could do it. I was not waiting in the wings for my 'big break!'

People ask me all the time, "How did you get started leading worship?"

The first time Pastor Brian Houston asked me to song lead - I nearly died and told him "No way - forget it." He had the WRONG person!

At the time I was the Vocal Director of our church and absolutely loved it! I loved to sing, especially in a backup role - but God had another plan. After about two years of trying to convince me, one day as Pastor Brian was leading the meeting, he just walked off and left it to me. It was just as well I didn't have anymore time to think about it because I was now doing it!

Three main roles of a worship leader:

1. We are there to lead the whole congregation into God's presence so that each one of them will be ministered to while spending time with the Father.

When I lead I always get a mental picture of God's arms outstretched and literally picking up and holding close, every single person in the auditorium. The mums and dads, the struggling teenagers, the elderly, the sick, the disheartened. God wants to speak into every one of their lives and my role is not to sing my favourite songs, and show off my voice, but to be a vessel for God to use to make it easier for the church and encourage them to 'lift Him up'.

2. We cover and lead the singers and musicians.

For years, our band and singers rehearsed without the worship leader. We don't do this anymore. You can't lead without knowledge. (well, you can, but you'll end up at the wrong place).

As a worship leader I must ensure I come to rehearsal prepared. I make sure I know how and where the worship should go. I have the music and charts, songlists etc ready to go. I work WITH the team when we are rehearsing. I need to love and understand the music team, and explain what I would like them to do, not expect them to guess!

3. We prepare the congregation for the preaching of the word.

As I have said, the more preparation you do, the more you have to give, to deposit into the people.

Have a deep conviction that is united with the leadership of the church. It is not about your spot and then the pastor's spot. Your role is to prepare the way, work the soil. Know where your pastor wants the service to go and do everything you can to help him get there.

Some keys I've learned.

From my experience as a worship leader, there have been some definite obstacles to overcome. Here are five keys which have helped me:

1. Preparation of songs.

When choosing songs for Sundays, I pay attention to a few things in particular. I go for songs that the congregation have really taken hold of and are really bringing life to the service. Because we write a lot of our own songs, our congregation have amazingly become so very musical - they are legends! I worked out that in Feb. '95 - Feb. '96 we introduced to them around 35 new songs and they are always hungry for more. We weave songs into each other, so that the flow is very natural, instead of start, stop, start, stop. Don't be scared to dwell on a song longer than planned if it is really working, be confident and communicate clearly to the team what you are doing.

When teaching new songs, I make sure the band and singers know what they are doing before we present it to the church. When melodies and structures are confused, it takes so much longer for your congregation to take hold of the songs.

2. Don't push

Sometimes, (especially at 8.30am in the morning) it is a little hard to get people going and to get them full of faith and vision for the service. Don't get angry, don't bully the people into worshipping God. Stay full of faith.

Faith isn't dependant on the circumstances. Even if the service seems flat, tired, and even can I say it - boring. Faith is living where you want to be. Lead from a position of faith. That means, I want the Holy Spirit here, I want the peoples' lives to be touched and changed. From a leadership perspective, you can't lead from the same position as the collective average congregation are at or, how the meeting feels. YOU NEED TO LEAD FROM THE FRONT!

So do I need to pretend or hype up the meeting?

3. You can't manufacture the Holy Spirit.

The Holy Spirit is not hype. Hype will only give you a temporary sense of feeling good. BUT it will not and cannot change peoples' lives or take them any closer to being like Jesus.

The Holy Spirit always has a purpose toward a long term result. Hype however is a very transient thing. Hype is excitement at one point in time, once you move from that point it just fades away. When the Holy Spirit moves on a meeting, He builds, refines, comforts, and is very pure. You can not replace or fake His prescence. Once the Holy Spirit gets hold of you, He will fire you up and you will be different from the inside out.

4. Communication.

We all need to be great communicators if we wish to be great leaders. This is an area I have really had to work on.

86

For example, have eye contact with the MD or the people who are following you. They cannot and should not have to predict your every move. The more you work with people, the more your friendships and confidence in each other's ability grows. When you develop communication skills, your understanding broadens, and this makes knowing where things are going a lot easier.

Practically speaking, I work closely with a couple of MD's in particular. Over the years they've learnt the way I like to lead, the different signals I use and my style. These relationships have certainly short-circuited unnecessary confusion.

5. Be yourself.

We are all created uniquely. We each have a definite purpose for our life and a definite 'flavour' in achieving this purpose.

As a singer, I find it easy to get people to sing! I try to stick to strong melody lines that most people can handle and not just make great music. Be accessible to everybody. Finding the key that unlocks the heart of every worshipper is my goal. I try to go with my strengths, to sing and encourage the church.

The big hurdle I came across was having to speak to the congregation - I would rather sing to millions than speak to a group of 20 people!!

I often remember getting up to lead worship and Pastor Brian would quickly say . . . "Just welcome people, would you, before you start?" Well, I would start to tremble, "Where's my husband?" I have to ask him what to say. I would write down on paper - 'HI CHURCH - WE ARE SO GLAD YOU'VE COME TONIGHT!'

I tried a few times to 'wing it', but when I opened my mouth, something really inspiring like 'LETS START' would come out!! I could recite hymns, poems, quote scriptures - but try and string six meaningful words together off the cuff was like writing a major essay!!

My pastors are such incredible communicators. Pat Mesiti only has to sneeze and people get saved!! I have physically had to work hard at it!! I even said yes to some speaking engagements to help build my confidence.

The first time I spoke at one of these engagements, the pastor said 'Well, at least you sang well!'

The second time, the pastors wife asked me 'Did you have any points?'

Get the picture? It has not come naturally to me.

I have given up many times, but God says again and again GET UP! Do what I've called you to do. So I persist. I listen to great speakers, read wonderful, inspiring books, and fight for the things that the enemy would love to steal from me.

Hebrews 10:35
"So do not lose the courage you had in the past, which has a great reward."

I've had some funny experiences leading worship. I remember once being so lost in worship with my eyes closed and hands raised that when I opened my eyes, I was facing the wrong way. And of course all the muso's were doubled up laughing at me.

Once, Geoff Bullock and I were travelling from Wellington, New Zealand to a conference in Palmerston North. We flew in an eight-seater plane and got caught in a storm. I would never have believed that a plane could be so tossed around. We were not only sick, but there was only one sick bag on board, for us to share!! (GROSS!!)

We landed and went directly to the church where the people were waiting for us. We ran up to the platform and started leading worship.

Halfway through the first song (we were feeling so-o-o-o sick), Geoff looked down his shirt front and there was vomit down his lapel!! (Lucky they all had their eyes shut).

Sometimes we minister only through faith in God and His ability, not ours (especially that day!!).

More than anything else, I know that God's heart is for His church, and for lost and hurting people to be found.

I can make mistakes, fall over, have a bad week, but if my heart is for God and His perfect plan, then His will will be done. I can do my very best and when God anoints it, I cannot fail.

CHAPTER FIVE

THE PROPHETIC SONG

You don't, need to bring forth 'new
revelation'
but TRUE <u>revelation</u> - from the
very heart of God.

Singers and players are often reluctant to step out and minister in prophetic song, because they may:

- Lack confidence.
- Be waiting for some super heavy word from God
- Just be a little scared of the unknown.

If the word of Christ is living within you and you are 'in tune' with what God is doing in and around you, then, you have all the ingredients for being a prophetic musician or singer .

You don't, need to bring forth 'new revelation' but TRUE revelation - from the very heart of God.

Many churches love to have the freedom to sing in the spirit, in almost free worship - to simply express themselves in other tongues or in English.

Musicians can worship on their instruments and enhance what God is doing.

You can use chord structures, simple melodies and key phrases from songs, playing one chord and just letting the people sing, or use no music at all. When the Holy Spirit turns up, He brings a sound all of His own.

To minister in the prophetic realm is a gift but not exclusive. It is accessible to any person in tune with God and desiring to grow in this area.

Sometimes in our rehearsals, we play and sing in the spirit. This helps to encourage and equip our team to operate and move under the anointing of the Holy Spirit. When we lead the congregation with confidence, they will follow.

Never let your organised music programme get in the way of what the Holy Spirit wants to do. This is always easier when you are operating as a team, looking to the leader for direction.

Don't be afraid or nervous about stepping out at the right time. God's Holy Spirit is gentle and kind. He will guide and help you.

Often the prophetic song or word that is brought forth is reflecting the preaching and direction set by your pastors. To use this time to stand in the middle of the congregation and air your own opinions and talents is very unwise. This is not a game we play.

God can and does speak to you wherever you are. When you build your relationship with Him and strengthen your foundations, your roots will grow deep and your tree will bear much fruit.

Colossians 1:9-10
"We pray that you will also have great wisdom and understanding in spiritual things so that you will live the kind of life that honours and pleases the Lord in every way. You will produce fruit in every good work and grow in the knowledge of God."

CHAPTER SIX

WORKING WITH YOUR SENIOR PASTOR

If Brian can get up, and move straight into his teaching, without having to prepare the people or build the atmosphere, then I have done my job well.

Here's my chance to spill the beans on Brian Houston.

Not really. Mark and I have been at Hills Christian Life Centre for ten years and we thank God for Brian and Bobbie who are incredible pastors!

It has been a great advantage being in Hills from the early days, growing in God and church vision alongside our pastors. We understand that we are all an integral part of the bigger picture and have the greater call of God on our lives.

Don't use every opportunity you spend with your Senior Pastor to discuss YOUR ministry and YOUR future. Get to know him, his thoughts, his vision for the church and what he expects from his team. Find out how you can best help him.

Develop a friendship. If Brian has to feel like he must be careful how he talks to me, not to offend etc, it makes it very hard. I would rather he be honest and then there are no 'mysteries'.

If he has to dance around my personality, it doesn't help me, the team, or the church. It doesn't help any situation if you are being super sensitive. Instead, it clouds the truth and gives the enemy some ground. The devil loves to destroy relationships. Stand firm, don't give him an inch!

Hebrews 13:17
Obey your leaders and act under their authority. they are watching over you, because they are responsible for your souls. Obey them so that they will do this work with joy, not sadness. It will not help you to make their work hard.

Be committed to your pastor's success in every area and be the first one to defend him on every level.

As worship pastor at our church, my goal is always to call God's presence into our services. When that happens, people can meet with Jesus with hearts that are ready and responsive to the Word as it is preached.

If Brian can get up, and move straight into his teaching, without having to prepare the people or build the atmosphere, then I have done my job well.

The more time you spend with your pastor, the easier communication and understanding will be between you.

Make sure they know you stand with them. Their job and responsibility is huge and they need to know their team will stand with them through thick and thin.

Your pastors are also human beings. Don't expect the world from them. Like you, they have good and bad days.

There will be differing opinions and times when you need to talk BUT you are there to serve and together you will be much more effective than you could ever be by yourself.

1 Peter 4:10
"Each of you has received a gift to use to serve others. Be good servants of God's various gifts of grace."

My pastor has seen things in me long before I ever did. He has pushed me to do things I never thought I could do, and has always been a strong support.

Most importantly, I trust his ability to hear from God. God's plan is perfect. That is good reason to sow my life into my church.

If you have no relationship with your pastor, start to build one. Go out for a coffee. Be determined to break down walls. Most conflicts are more imaginary than real.

You are running the same race, run it together.

CONCLUSION

Philippians 3:12-14

"I do not mean that I am already as God wants me to be. I have not yet reached that goal, but I continue trying to reach it and to make it mine. Christ wants me to do that, which is the reason He made me His. Brothers and sisters, I know that I have not yet reached that goal, but there is one thing I always do. Forgetting the past and straining toward what is ahead, I keep trying to reach the goal and get the prize for which God called me through Christ to the life above."

Worship God with all your heart, all your soul and all your mind. Give Him your talents, dreams and desires, and as you serve you will know fulfillment, peace and joy, that only comes through relationship with Jesus Christ.

Live to worship Him.

BIBLIOGRAPHY

Scriptures quoted from The Holy Bible, New Century Version. Copyright © 1987, 1988,1991 Word Publishing, Dallas, Texas 75039. Used by permission.

Scripture quotations from THE MESSAGE. Copyright © by Eugene H Peterson 1993, 1994, 1995. Used by permission of NavPress Publishing Group.

Scripture quotations from The Open Bible New Amerian Standard. Copyright © The Lockman Foundation 1960, 1962, 1963, 1968, 1971, 1972, 1973, 1975, 1977. La Habra, California.